HOUSEPLANT
~ SUCCESS ~

An essential guide to growing beautiful plants
in your home, with 165 photographs

JACKIE MATTHEWS

LORENZ BOOKS

This edition is published by Lorenz Books
an imprint of Anness Publishing Ltd
Blaby Road, Wigston, Leicestershire LE18 4SE
info@anness.com

www.lorenzbooks.com; www.annesspublishing.com

If you like the images in this book and would like to investigate using
them for publishing, promotions or advertising, please visit our website
www.practicalpictures.com for more information.

Publisher: Joanna Lorenz
Editor: Valerie Ferguson
Photography: John Freeman and Michelle Garrett
Text contributors: John Clinch, Gilly Love and Peter McHoy
Series Designer: Larraine Shamwana
Designer: Ian Sandom
Production Controller: Pirong Wang

Additional photographs: The Garden Picture Library,
p. 43 top left; p. 50 top left. Peter McHoy, p. 34 bottom left.

A CIP catalogue record for this book
is available from the British Library.

PUBLISHER'S NOTE
Although the advice and information in this book are believed to be accurate and
true at the time of going to press, neither the authors nor the publisher can
accept any legal responsibility or liability for any errors or omissions that may
have been made nor for any inaccuracies nor for any loss, harm or injury that
comes about from following instructions or advice in this book.

CONTENTS

Introduction

HOUSEPLANTS CAN INSTANTLY CHANGE THE ATMOSPHERE OF ANY ROOM IN YOUR HOME. BEFORE YOU BUY, THOUGH, YOU NEED TO DECIDE HOW FLOWERING AND FOLIAGE PLANTS WILL WORK IN SITU AND HOW TO KEEP THEM LOOKING THEIR BEST.

Left: Given the right conditions, plants will flourish in your home.

GROWING HOUSEPLANTS

Generally, most plants are easy to look after if they are provided with the right conditions, especially light, moisture and nutrition. If well tended they will look attractive, often varying their appearance with seasonal flowers or colourful bracts. Those plants that require exacting conditions not normally found in a home will be high maintenance, and could become a chore to look after, so you

Above: Pot plants in flower will add colour and warmth to a room.

may prefer to choose from the wide selection of plants that are easy to care for and require minimum attention.

Most indoor collections found in garden centres and florists consist of a combination of easy-care, long-lasting foliage plants and seasonal plants. Flowering pot plants are often regarded as short-term colour, more like long-lasting cut flowers, but with careful pruning, deadheading and feeding, some can be treated as perennials and will flower again the following year.

HUMIDITY

The amount of heat and light in your home is major consideration. The dry heat caused by central heating can be damaging. Tropical plants especially require moisture in the atmosphere. Fortunately, the majority of houseplants can survive in low levels of humidity, particularly in summer when windows are open. In winter, when heating is turned up, commercial room humidifiers will moisten the air, but a more economic solution would be to select plants that do not need very humid conditions.

Above: Change the colour scheme of a room by introducing a bold group of plants.

ACHIEVING DIFFERENT EFFECTS

Plants can entirely change the atmosphere of a room, or introduce a new mood or even colour scheme from season to season. Fragrant spring bulbs, pots of herbs, autumnal toned chrysanthemums or a bowl of brightly coloured cyclamen will all add to the mood of their particular time of year.

Some plants are better suited to certain types of interiors than others, and should be compatible in size and shape as well as colour. Small plants that complement fabrics and wallpapers work well with a traditional, cottagey décor. Stark modern interiors can take big, bold "architectural" plants. Be prepared to invest in one or two really good specimens if necessary because they have far more impact than half a dozen cheaper plants.

SHOPPING FOR HOUSEPLANTS

Plants are living, perishable things, and supplies often fluctuate widely according to season and what the commercial growers decide to market.

Whenever possible, buy where the plants are well cared for in surroundings conducive to good growth: warmth, freedom from icy blasts, high humidity (though this is not important for cacti and succulents), and a high level of diffused light or artificial lighting designed for plant growth. Wilting, diseased or dying plants should not be on display.

Look beneath the pot – some roots will have grown through if capillary matting has been used for watering, but masses of long roots indicate that the plant needs to be repotted. Always check the plant for signs of pests and diseases. Turn over one or two of the leaves – pests may be lurking out of sight.

With flowering plants, timing is everything. You may get several weeks of pleasure if you buy a plant just coming into flower rather than one that is already at its peak.

GARDENER'S TIP
Houseplants tend to grow slowly and are cultivated in a range of sizes. If a room requires a large plant, select one at the right height or slightly smaller than required. Otherwise, you could wait a long time for a 90 cm (3 ft) specimen to reach the necessary size.

Left: Mauve flowers look very effective against a light grey or pale blue wall.

Below: Plants benefit from being placed in strong but indirect light. It is a good idea to move them occasionally if light is low.

COLOUR

Houseplants come in every possible colour. Even foliage comes in many shades of green, in variegated forms, and with silver or bronze tints. Plants can be used to add colour or to complement different decorative schemes.

Heavy, dark green foliage, distinctive in itself, would dominate a softly toned wallpaper or delicate paint effect. Conversely, pale fern fronds or a pastel-and-white flowering plant would enhance a soft colour scheme. While most plants would complement pale plain-coloured walls,

placing foliage or flowering plants in front of a patterned wallpaper or furnishings, especially a floral design, could be problematic. If you have patterned paper or fabric, take a piece with you when you buy plants to help you select a complementary green.

SUN AND GOOD LIGHT

In a typical house it is usually difficult to give houseplants enough light for really healthy and even growth, yet ironically a position on a windowsill in full sun will probably injure or kill most of them. Sun through unshaded glass is much more intense than sun in the open – it acts like a magnifying glass and will often scorch vulnerable foliage. Although most plants will benefit from gentler early and late sun, when the intensity is not too great,

---

SUN-LOVING PLANTS

Ananas
Coleus
Pelargonium
Roses, miniature
Yucca elephantipes

PLANTS FOR SHADE

Asplenium nidus
Dracaena
Fatsia
Hedera helix
Philodendron

---

you need really tough sun-lovers to tolerate the hot midday sun intensified through glass.

Most cacti and succulents are ideal for a windowsill position. *Echinocactus, ferocactus, opuntias, parodias* and *rebutias* are all readily available.

Succulents such as *lithops* and *kalanchoes* are also excellent for hot windowsills. There is more variation in shape and growth habit among succulents than cacti, but if you want yet more variety there are other true sun-lovers you can try.

Some plants that benefit from softer winter sun may be harmed by the harsher summer sun that will scorch tender leaves.

SHADE

Plants that tolerate lower light levels are especially useful. They can be positioned by shady windows and within any room, perhaps on a table or sideboard, and still survive for a reasonable time. You can use any plant in these conditions, but after a while most will become sickly and deteriorate. You will then have to move them into better light or buy a new plant.

FOLIAGE

Purely foliage plants are anything but dull. Leaves come in a vast range of greens, many are variegated, some are more colourful than many flowers, and all last much longer. Many also have contrasting textures and shapes.

> **FOLIAGE PLANTS**
> *Aglaonema hybrids*
> *Asparagus densiflorus 'sprengeri'*
> *Begonia, foliage*
> *Dracaena marginata*
> *Fatsia japonica*
> *Ficus benjamina 'Starlight'*
> *Hedera helix,* variegated
> *Monstera deliciosa*
> *Philodendron scandens*
> *Sansevieria trifasciata 'Laurentii'*
> *Syngonium podophyllum*
> *Yucca elephantipes*

Plants grown for their leaves will form the backbone of most arrangements and groupings. They can also form a backdrop for flowers.

SHAPE

Interesting shape will compensate for any lack of colour in a leaf. Plants such as philodendrons and ficus, *F. benjamina* create as much interest as those with bright flowers or brilliant foliage, and they do it in a restrained way that creates the right mood for a room.

Above: *A selection of plants showing interesting foliage and texture.*

7

Introduction

TEXTURE

Leaf texture adds variety. There are rough, hairy and puckered leaves, all of which can add extra interest and contrast to a group. Some demand to be touched, providing tactile as well as visual stimulation.

RELIABLE FLOWERING PLANTS

Aechmea fasciata
Begonia, elatior type
Chrysanthemum
Clivia miniata
Exacum affine
Hydrangea
Jasminum polyanthum
Kalanchoe
Pelargonium, Regal
Primula obconica
Saintpaulia
Stephanotis floribunda
Tillandsia cynea
Vriesea

FLOWERING PLANTS

Houseplants with flowers are usually a little more difficult than foliage plants to keep long-term. However, they add brilliance and colour that even the boldest foliage plants find difficult to match, and some have the extra bonus of fragrance.

A few flowering plants are available throughout the year (*chrysanthemums, kalanchoes* and *saintpaulias* are examples), but most flower in a particular season. This is no bad thing because it prevents your displays becoming predictable or boring. Some are annuals, or treated as annuals, and have to be discarded when flowering is over. These short-term flowering pot plants are especially useful for creating instant displays of stunning colour anywhere in the home. They also make it possible to continue a colour scheme throughout the year using different plants.

SCENT

Houseplants allow you to enjoy natural fragrances the year round. Sometimes a single, strongly scented plant is sufficient for an entire room. You will need several in succession, but this gives you the chance to enjoy different kinds of perfume over the seasons.

Above: *Flowering houseplants may need more care, but they give so much pleasure with their colourful blooms and bright green foliage.*

GARDENER'S TIP

Some flowers give heady perfume which can be overpowering, depending on your sensitivity. To make sure you will enjoy their fragrance over the full flowering period, try to buy new plants just as they are coming into bloom.

For late winter and early spring there are numerous varieties of scented hyacinths and narcissi. During autumn, plant up individual pots with hyacinths every fortnight to give you fragrance in late winter.

In summer, many shrubs and plants provide scent. Aromatic pelargoniums (geraniums) start flowering in late spring and will continue into autumn, if placed on a sunny windowsill. You will need several together to make an impact, and grow them where you will brush their leaves as you pass.

Some lilies provide a concentrated perfume from late afternoon into the evening. Plant specially prepared bulbs at intervals during winter to provide scented blooms from summer into autumn.

How This Book Works

In this book you will find practical advice on choosing plants that will best suit you and your home. *Getting Started* covers basic tools and equipment, *Caring for Houseplants* provides advice on looking after plants, while *Troubleshooting* discusses pests and diseases. The *A–Z of Houseplants*

Above: A miniature rose provides both colour and fragrance.

describes approximately a hundred essential houseplants and their cultural requirements. *Displays & Groupings* suggests ways to show off your plants, and *The Right Plant for the Right Place* explains which plants are best suited to the different environments created by key rooms in the home. Finally, *Plants at Their Best* names those with seasonal interest, and is followed by a list of the common names of plants mentioned in this book.

SCENTED PLANTS

Hoya bella
Gardenia jasminoides
Hyacinthus
Jasminum officinale
Lilium (oriental hybrids)
Narcissus
Stephanotis floribunda

Getting Started

ONCE YOU HAVE DECIDED WHICH PLANTS YOU WANT TO GROW, YOU
NEED TO STOCK UP ON BASIC TOOLS AND EQUIPMENT, INCLUDING THE
CORRECT SOIL FOR POTTING, AND TO CHOOSE THE APPROPRIATE
CONTAINERS TO DISPLAY YOUR PLANTS TO BEST ADVANTAGE.

TOOLS AND EQUIPMENT

You can look after your houseplants without any special tools. An old kitchen fork
and spoon are amazingly versatile, and
some real enthusiasts manage with a jug
from the kitchen cupboard instead of a
proper watering-can. However, the right
tools do make the jobs easier, and usually
more pleasant. The tools described here
won't cost much. Take particular care over
the choice of a watering-can and a mister –
both should be in daily use, so don't skimp
on these.

Canes (stakes) – usually made from
bamboo, used for supporting plants.

Dibber – a tool used for making a hole in
potting soil.

Fertilizer – food for plants, which comes in
various forms.

Knife – useful for taking cuttings and other
indoor gardening tasks.

Leaf shines – products for putting a shine
on glossy leaves.

Leaf-wipes – tissue-type leaf shine.

Mister – a sprayer producing a fine mist.

Insecticide – for pest control.

Insecticidal plant pins – insecticide-impreg-
nated strips to push into potting soil.

Raffia – a natural tying material.

Rooting hormone – stimulates root
formation on cuttings.

Scissors – useful for cutting ties and
deadheading etc.

Water indicator – indicates moisture level
in soil.

Watering-can, indoor – one with a long,
narrow spout for precision watering.

Wire – plastic-coated to protect stems.

Mister

Various
pots

Watering-can

Leaf-wipes

Water
indicator

Raffia

Insecticide

Leaf
shines

Plastic coated wire

Rooting
hormone

Knife

Scissors

Fertilizers

Insecticidal plant pin

Dibber

Canes (stakes)

POTTING SOIL

The use of an appropriate potting soil can make all the difference to successful indoor gardening. It will provide vital nutrients essential for growth, and act as a reservoir for moisture.

Loam-based (soil-based) – potting soil is heavier and less pleasant to handle than peat-based (peat-moss) versions, but it may be the best choice for some plants. Tall or large plants that tend

Loam-based (soil-based) soil

to be top-heavy may benefit from the extra weight in the pot. Some plants, including most succulents, benefit from the good drainage and reserve of nutrients provided by loam-based soil.

Peat-based (peat moss) mixtures – light and easy to handle, but usually require supplementary feeding after a month or so. They can dry out more completely

Peat-based (peat-moss) soil

than loam and become difficult to re-wet, and they are more easily overwatered. They can vary greatly in quality, so when you have found one that is satisfactory, it is a good idea to stick to it. Some gardeners are reluctant to use peat-based products on the grounds of depleting wetland areas. Alternative products are available, including mixes based on coir (waste from coconuts).

Orchid mixtures – are unlike any others that you will use. They are free-draining and contain no loam (soil). Bark is a common ingredient.

Orchid mixture

Cactus soils – very free-draining, and will contain plenty of grit or other material to ensure that the roots don't become waterlogged.

Cactus soil

Ericaceous potting soils – for acid-loving, or lime-hating, plants such as azaleas. Lime or other alkaline materials are not used in the mixture, and the pH is more acidic than in normal soils.

Water-absorbing granules – sometimes used as an additive to potting soil. They swell when wet and hold many times their own weight of water. They can be useful if you are often away for a few days and find it difficult to water regularly.

Fine gravel - helps with drainage if mixed with the soil when potting up a plant, and can be used as an attractive mulch on the surface of the soil to prevent your plant drying out as quickly.

Fine gravel

CHOOSING POTS AND CONTAINERS

Pots and containers can form part of the room décor just like a vase or ornament. The right container will enhance an attractive plant and can often compensate for a mediocre one. Part of the fun of growing houseplants is displaying them with imagination. Many everyday items can be used, and searching for containers can be part of the enjoyment of growing houseplants.

The bigger the plant, the smaller the pot or container should be in relationship to it. Small, bushy plants look best in pots that are either roughly their size or smaller. A tall plant, 25–60 cm (10–24 in) in height, looks best in a pot about a quarter of its height. The pot must also be sufficiently heavy to provide a solid base when the soil dries out, otherwise the plant might topple over.

Half pots, which stand about half the height of ordinary pots but have the same diameter, suit cacti which do not have a large root system, as well as azaleas.

GALVANIZED METAL CONTAINERS AND CACHE-POTS

These have a waterproof base and no drainage holes. They are useful for flowering plants that are on display for a short time only and for fast-growing plants that require frequent repotting.

The disadvantage is that you do need to be careful about watering. Make sure that the plant pot is easily lifted out for watering or place on a bed of crocks or stones.

GLASS

These containers allow for imaginative presentation. You can surround the plant pot with visually attractive material such as coloured stones, marbles, sand or a thick layer of moss or pine cones. Hyacinths look particularly attractive in glass containers.

PLANTERS AND SELF-WATERING CONTAINERS

Large containers are ideal for displaying a group of plants. Some planters are self-

Below: Many types of container are suitable for houseplants.

Glazed ceramic

Terracotta

Planters

watering with a reservoir at the bottom, which means you can leave several days between watering. Plants generally thrive in these.

BASKETS

Many plants look especially attractive in wicker, moss-covered or wire baskets. If you use a basket not specifically intended for plants, line it with a protective sheet of flexible plastic, otherwise water will seep through and spoil the surface underneath. The plastic should not be visible once the basket has been planted.

Ordinary hanging baskets are unsuitable for using indoors because of the problems with drips. Choose one with a drip tray or water reservoir.

TERRACOTTA

Large terracotta pots and containers are good for specimen plants. The weight gives essential stability to plants with thin trunks and wide, arching branches.

The orange tone of natural terracotta can be softened by weathering it outside over winter. Or it can be artificially aged by applying a weak solution of a pale-coloured, water-based paint.

Match the drip tray to the pot and make sure that it is internally glazed, otherwise water will seep through and spoil the surface it is resting on. For a plant that requires humidity, choose a drip tray large enough to take stones or water-retaining granules as well as the plant pot.

GLAZED CERAMIC

Now available in a wide choice of solid and patterned colours. Solid colours are more versatile than patterns and are useful for linking a plant's foliage with a room's colour scheme.

Many glazed containers do not have drainage holes; to overcome this, quarter-fill a large one with pebbles, cover with a thin layer of charcoal and top with potting soil.

Wire baskets

Wicker basket

Galvanized metal pail

Caring for Houseplants

IF YOU WANT LUSH, HEALTHY HOUSEPLANTS YOU MUST CARE FOR THEM ROUTINELY AND APPLY REMEDIAL TREATMENT AS SOON AS A PROBLEM OCCURS. TO INCREASE AND REJUVENATE YOUR STOCK, SOME PROPAGATION TECHNIQUES WILL BE USEFUL.

WATERING

Some plants will require watering daily, others perhaps once or twice a week. In winter, some may not need water for weeks on end. Don't water just because a moisture meter or indicator tells you the potting soil is dry. Cacti and succulents resting during winter, for example, should not be kept constantly moist.

Feel the surface of the soil and water when the soil has dried out but before the plant is affected by lack of water. Don't allow the pot to stand in surplus water as this will waterlog the soil. Most plants do, however, appreciate being stood in a deep sink or bucket of water for 30 minutes before being drained and returned to their original position.

Above: Choose a watering-can with a long, narrow spout so that you can control the flow easily. You want the water around the roots, not over the leaves (or on your table or windowsill).

HUMIDITY

Raising the humidity level will benefit most plants, except sun-lovers. Covering the soil surface with moss, stones or shells will reduce water evaporation. Placing plants on wet pebbles immediately raises the level of humidity around a plant; make sure the roots are not in contact with the water.

Misting plants daily will give a better texture to the leaves and help keep them free of dust, as well as improving humidity for a short time. Use tepid water and ideally mist your plants in the morning so the leaves dry before nightfall.

FEEDING

Slow-release fertilizers feed a plant over a period of months, while controlled-release types release the fertilizer only when the soil is above a temperature suitable for most plants' active growth. Granules can be mixed before potting; pellets or sticks can be pushed into the soil around an established plant. Liquid feeds make it easier to stop feeding when the plant is resting. Some are applied regularly, others less often.

VACATION CARE

Your vacation may not be good news for your plants if a friend or neighbour cannot take care of the watering for you. Fortunately, there are plenty of ways to help your plants through this period of potential stress.

Above: Group plants together in a tray or large container and water thoroughly before you go away, leaving a little water in the bottom of the outer container.

Move your plants into a few large groups in a cool position out of direct sunlight. Stand them on a tray of gravel, watered to just below the level of the pot bases. This will not moisten the potting soil, but the humid air will help to keep the plants in good condition.

Supply all the most vulnerable plants with some kind of watering system. There are various proprietary devices on sale, but many of these are suitable if you have a few plants only.

Porous reservoirs and ceramic mushrooms are both simple, effective systems, but you need one for each pot.

Wicks, which are inserted into pots placed above a reservoir of water, are suitable for a handful of plants.

Drip feeds, sold for greenhouse and garden use, are good, but expensive.

CAPILLARY MATTING

You can use capillary matting, sold for greenhouse benches, in the sink or the bath. The system works best with plastic pots that have nothing placed over the drainage holes. Water the plants thoroughly before placing on the matting.

For the sink, cut a length of matting to fit the draining area but long enough to reach the bottom of the sink. Fill the sink with water, or leave the plug out but let a tap drip on to the mat to keep it moist. If you do the latter, have a trial run to make sure that it keeps the mat moist without wasting water. Do the same for the bath, but if you leave water in it, place the mat and plants on a plank of wood on bricks.

Above: Capillary wicks will draw water from a reservoir. Make sure the wicks are soaked and put one end deeply into the potting soil. The other end must reach the reservoir base.

GROOMING

Regular grooming of your plants will keep them looking good. Apart from picking off dead flowers, which is best done whenever you notice them, grooming is only a once-a-week task. Most jobs need doing less frequently than this, but by making a routine of tidying up your plants you will almost certainly detect pests, diseases and nutritional problems that much earlier.

DEADHEADING

Removing flowers as they fade not only keeps the plant looking neat, but in many cases encourages the production of more flowers. It also discourages diseases; many fungal infections start on dead flowers. Apart from flower spikes, remove the stalks as well as the flowers, using a pulling and twisting motion at the same time. Cut whole flower heads or spikes back to just above a pair of leaves.

FOLIAGE

Remove dying and fallen leaves. These will spoil the appearance of a plant and can harbour disease. Most can be pulled off with a gentle tug, but tough ones may have to be cut off.

Dust settles on foliage just as it does everywhere else, and it can prevent the plant from breathing properly and block light. If the leaves are delicate or hairy dust them using a soft paintbrush.

Large, glossy leaves can be wiped clean using a soft damp cloth or sponge or proprietary leaf-wipes. Plants with small glossy leaves may have too many to make the use of leaf-wipes a sensible option. Stand these outside in a shower of light rain in the summer or spray them with water. In winter, plants small enough to be handled in this way can simply have their leaves swished gently in a bowl of tepid water.

1 Plants with large, glossy leaves can be wiped clean. Commercially produced leaf-wipes are convenient to use, but check that they don't carry a warning against using them on certain plants.

2 Cacti, succulents and plants with hairy leaves such as *saintpaulias* are much more difficult to clean. These should be brushed carefully with a soft paintbrush kept for the purpose to remove dust.

PRUNING

You can improve the shape of many house-plants by pinching out the growing tips to prevent them from becoming tall and leggy. Removing the tips of the shoots makes the plant bushier. *Hedera*, *hypoestes*, *pileas* and *tradescantias* are among the many plants that benefit from this treatment. Beware of doing it to slow-growing plants.

Start when the plants are young, and repeat it whenever the growth looks too thin and long. This is especially useful for trailers such as *tradescantias*: a dense cascade about 30 cm (12 in) long will look better than weedy-looking shoots twice the length.

Right: Train new growth of climbing plants before it becomes difficult to bend. Twist stems carefully into position to avoid breaking tender shoots.

If any all-green shoots develop on a varie-gated plant, prune to the point of origin.

Climbers and trailers need regular attention. Tie in any new shoots to the support, and cut off any long ones.

Pruning can also be a good opportunity for propagating your houseplants, as longer shoots can be treated as cuttings to pot up for new plants.

Above: If you want a bushy rather than a tall or sprawling plant, pinch out the growing tips a few times while it is still young. This will stimulate the growth of sideshoots and produce a bushier effect.

GARDENER'S TIP

Pests and diseases can spread more easily and rapidly from plant to plant when they are in close proximity, and you may be less likely to notice early symptoms on leaves hidden by other plants. Make grooming a regular routine to minimize the danger.

REPOTTING PLANTS

Sooner or later most plants need repotting, and it can give an ailing plant a new lease of life. But not all plants respond well to frequent repotting, and some prefer to be in small pots. Knowing when to repot, and into which size, comes with experience.

Repotting a plant should be considered on an annual basis, but not actually done unless the plant needs it. Young plants require it much more frequently than older ones. Once a large specimen is in a big pot it may be better to keep it growing by repotting into another pot of the same size, by topdressing, or simply by additional feeding when required.

WHEN TO REPOT

The sight of roots growing through the base does not indicate that repotting is necessary. Check by inverting the pot and knocking the rim on a hard surface while supporting the plant and soil with your hand. It is normal for some roots to run around the inside, but if there is also a solid mass of roots it is time to pot on.

Above: A plant with tightly packed roots needs to be potted on.

HOW TO REPOT

1 Prepare a pot that is one or two sizes larger than the original. Cover the drainage hole of a clay pot with pieces of broken pot. Don't cover the holes in a plastic pot that you intend using with a capillary watering mat.

2 Place a small amount of potting soil in the base of the new pot. Knock out the root-ball from the pre-watered plant and position it so that it is at the right height.

3 Trickle potting soil around the sides, turning the pot. Gently firm the soil with your fingers. Make sure there is a gap of about 1–2.5 cm (½–1 in) between the top of the compost and the rim of the pot. Water thoroughly. Place in the shade for about a week and mist the leaves daily.

SIMPLE PROPAGATION

In the late spring and summer it is possible to multiply some of your plants by means of simple propagation. It is usually best to do this in spring or early summer. Always take several cuttings from the plant in case some fail.

STEM CUTTINGS

By far the easiest method is from stem cuttings. Ivy, *tradescantia* and *Sparrmannia africana* (house lime) are just some of the plants that may be propagated this way. Choose a piece of stem 7.5–13 cm (3–5 in) long and cut just below a leaf. Make the cut straight, not at an angle, using a razor blade or sharp knife. Remove most of the leaves from the lower half of the cutting. Stand the cutting in a glass of water in a light position, making sure no leaves are in contact with the water. Pot up the cutting when the new roots are 2.5–4 cm (1–1½in) long. Change the water as necessary.

The Swiss cheese plant and many philodendrons can become straggly with age. They can be divided into several plants by taking stem cuttings with noticeable root nodules at their bases. Place them in water in good light as before.

PLANTLETS

The tiny plantlets produced by some plants, including spider plants, mother of thousands and piggyback plants, can be inserted directly into soil or can be rooted in water as for stem cuttings. Wait until a good root system has developed before potting up.

LEAF CUTTINGS

Saintpaulias, leaf begonias and many succulents are propagated by leaf cuttings.

1 Cut a mature leaf, with about 5 cm (2 in) of stalk attached from the base of a plant. Make a straight cut using a sharp knife.

2 Fill a pot with a rooting medium and make a hole using a pencil or dibber at a 45-degree angle. Insert the cutting with the back of the leaf towards the outside of the pot and the base just above the soil. Press gently around the stalk, then water.

3 Position short canes close to the leaf and place an airtight plastic bag over the pot. Secure with a rubber band. Place in a light position avoiding direct sunlight as this might scorch vulnerable leaves.

Troubleshooting

REGULAR INSPECTION OF YOUR PLANTS WILL ALERT YOU TO ANY SERIOUS PROBLEMS, DISEASE OR INFESTATIONS IN TIME TO TAKE THE NECESSARY REMEDIAL ACTION.

PHYSICAL PROBLEMS

Upper Leaves Turn Yellow: affects lime-hating plants, and is caused by watering with hard water containing too much calcium. Use boiled or filtered water only.

Brown Spots or Patches on Leaves: may be due to insect infestation, too much direct sunlight or splashing water on leaves.

Leaves Curling at the Edges and Dropping: can be caused by too cool an atmosphere, overwatering or cold draught.

Brown Tips and Edges to Leaves: usually too little humidity and too much direct sun. Can be due to either overwatering or overfeeding.

Wilting Leaves: underwatering, or if soil is waterlogged, then overwatering. In this case the roots will have rotted.

Dull Leaves: Lifeless leaves may simply require a wipe with a damp cloth to remove dust and grime. May also indicate too much light or the presence of red spider mites.

Sudden Leaf Fall: may occur after repotting or when a plant has been moved to a new location. Can be the result of a sharp rise or fall in temperature, an icy draught or underwatering.

No Flowers: usually caused by insufficient light. If the flower buds develop but drop before opening, this is probably due to dry air or underwatering. Flowers that develop but fade quickly may be getting too much heat, too little light and not enough water.

Variegated Leaves Turning Green: due to lack of light, which generally results in pale, small leaves and a leggy growing habit.

Rotting Leaves and Stems: probably due to a disease and often caused by overwatering, poor drainage and providing insufficient ventilation for the plant.

Discoloration of Clay Pots: a green slimy film on pots indicates overwatering or poor drainage. A white crust is due either to using hard water or overfeeding.

Left: If the potting soil has become very dry, with a hard surface, loosen the surface with a fork to help a dried-out root-ball absorb water.

PESTS AND DISEASES

Mealy Bug: small insects covered with white fluff that form colonies in leaves and in leaf axils. Eventually leaves turn yellow, wilt and drop off. Wipe off the bugs with alcohol-impregnated swabs, or you can spray with malathion.

Vine Weevil: a creamy-coloured grub that lives in the soil and eats roots. The adult dark brown beetle chews leaves. If caught early, leaves and soil need spraying with pesticide.

Whitefly: tiny, moth-like flies that deposit a sticky honeydew on the undersides of leaves, encouraging black mould to develop. Spray with malathion or pyrethrum every three days.

Above: Whitefly damage houseplants and look unsightly. They proliferate quickly, so take prompt action to remove them.

Red Spider Mites: red or pink eight-legged pests that suck the sap, causing black spots and yellowed leaves. Barely visible to the eye, infestation is indicated by the presence of fine webs and mottling of the plant's leaves. Remove affected leaves and spray with malathion or other insecticide.

Aphids (Greenfly): brown, grey or green insects that suck the sap, leaving sticky honeydew which causes leaves to wither. Remove pests with alcohol-impregnated swabs, then spray with a pesticide.

Powdery Mildew: coats the leaves with a white powdery deposit. Remove and destroy affected leaves and spray with a systemic fungicide. Improve the ventilation.

Black Leg (Black Stem Rot): affects stem cuttings, turning the bases black. Remove and destroy affected cuttings. Use a light, well-draining medium and dip cuttings in a fungicide hormone-rooting powder.

Sooty Mould (Black Mold): fungus that often grows on honeydew left by aphids and mealy bugs. Wipe off the mould using well-diluted soapy water. Eradicate insects.

Botrytis (Grey Mold): caused by growing plants in a cool, damp atmosphere with poor air circulation. Remove affected parts and spray with a systemic fungicide. Move plants to a warmer location.

Above: If whitefly or aphid infestation is mild you may be able to reduce the population by swishing the plant in water.

A–Z of Houseplants

MOST OF THE HOUSEPLANTS IN THE FOLLOWING PAGES CAN BE FOUND IN GARDEN CENTRES AND SHOPS. THE SELECTION COVERS FLOWERING, FOLIAGE AND SCENTED VARIETIES.

ACALYPHA HISPIDA

Tall and quick-growing foliage plant with long red tassel-like flowers, in autumn. 'Alba': white flowers.

Temperature: winter 15°C (59°F).
Humidity: high humidity. Mist frequently if room is centrally heated.
Position: good light, not direct sun.
Watering and feeding: never let soil dry out. Feed from spring to autumn.
Care: deadhead. Prune by half in early spring or late summer. Repot in spring or topdress if in large pot.
Propagation: cuttings.

ACHIMENES HYBRIDS

Short-lived flowers, in pink, purple, yellow, red or white, through summer. Dormant over winter.

Temperature: undemanding when dormant; minimum 13°C (55°F) while it is growing.
Humidity: mist developing flower buds then provide humidity without spraying by standing plant on a tray of wet pebbles.
Position: good light, not direct sun.
Watering and feeding: water with tepid, soft water during growing season, keeping soil moist. Feed regularly.
Care: support the stems or grow in a hanging pot. Stop watering when leaves begin to drop. Leave rhizomes in pot or store in peat or sand in frost-free place. Start into growth or replant in late winter or early spring.
Propagation: division of rhizomes; cuttings; seed (not named varieties).

AECHMEA FASCIATA

Bromeliad with banded foliage. Long-lasting, spiky blue flowers fading to lilac with pink bracts, mid-summer to early winter.

Temperature: winter minimum 15°C (59°F).
Humidity: undemanding.
Position: good light, not direct sun.

Watering and feeding: keep roots moist. Top up water in funnel in summer, but empty it in winter. Feed with weak fertilizer in summer.
Care: mist only on hot days. To stimulate mature plant into flower, enclose in plastic bag with two ripe apples for a few days. Main plant will die after flowering, but produces offsets.
Propagation: offsets (remove when about half height of parent).

AGLAONEMA HYBRIDS

Tolerant clump-forming foliage plants with silvery-grey variegations.
Temperature: winter minimum 15°C (59°F).
Humidity: high humidity. Mist regularly.
Position: Light shade, not direct sun.
Watering and feeding: water freely from spring to autumn, sparingly in winter. Feed from spring to autumn.
Care: repot only when necessary.
Propagation: cuttings; division.

ALOE VARIEGATA

Trouble-free succulents with thick fleshy, banded leaves, occasionally red flowers.
Temperature: cool but frost-free in winter, 5°C (41°F).
Humidity: will tolerate dry air.

Position: full sun.
Watering and feeding: water twice a week in summer. Feed occasionally in summer.
Care: repot in spring every second year.
Propagation: offsets; seed in spring.

ANANAS BRACTEATUS STRIATUS

Foliage bromeliads with spiky, brightly striped, cream-and-pink leaves.
Temperature: winter 15–18°C (59–64°F).
Humidity: undemanding, but mist in very hot weather.
Position: good light. Variegation often better in sun.
Watering and feeding: water freely in summer, cautiously in winter. Feed from spring to autumn.
Care: in summer, occasionally add a little water to the leaf "vase". Encourage mature plants to flower by placing in a plastic bag with ripe apples or bananas.
Propagation: leaf crown on top of fruit.

ANTHURIUM SCHERZERIANUM
Distinctive foliage plant with exotic red blooms spring to late summer.

Temperature: winter minimum 16°C (60°F).
Humidity: high humidity. Mist frequently, avoiding flowers.
Position: good light, not direct summer sun.
Watering and feeding: water freely in summer, sparingly in winter. Soft water if possible. Feed with weak fertilizer in summer.
Care: repot every second year, in spring, using fibrous potting mixture.
Propagation: division.

ASPARAGUS DENSIFLORUS 'SPRENGERI'
Fern-like foliage on arching to pendulous, thread-like stems.

Temperature: winter minimum 7°C (45°F).
Humidity: mist occasionally, especially in centrally heated room.
Position: good light or partial shade, not direct sun.
Watering and feeding: water from spring to autumn, sparingly in winter. Feed from spring to early autumn.
Care: cut back by half if turns yellow or grows too large. Repot young plants every spring, older ones every second spring.
Propagation: division; seed.

ASPIDISTRA ELATIOR
Evergreen herbaceous plant with large dark green leaves growing directly from soil. Tough constitution. 'Variegata': creamy white longitudinal stripes.
Temperature: keep cool, 7–10°C (45–50°F) is ideal.
Humidity: tolerates dry air.
Position: light or shade, but avoid exposing to direct sun.
Watering and feeding: water moderately from spring to autumn, sparingly in winter. Feed from spring to early autumn.
Care: wash or sponge leaves occasionally to remove dust and improve light penetration. Repot when necessary – every three or four years.
Propagation: division.

ASPLENIUM

Useful ferns. *A. bulbiferum*: ferny fronds, small plantlets on mature leaves. *A. nidus*: glossy, undivided leaves forming vase-like rosette, very tolerant.

Temperature: winter minimum: *A. bulbiferum* 13°C (55°F); *A. nidus* 16°C (60°F)
Humidity: high humidity.
Position: shade.
Watering and feeding: water freely from spring to autumn, moderately in winter. Soft water if possible.
Care: dust *A. nidus* periodically. Trim off any brown edges.
Propagation: division; pot up plantlets of *A. bulbiferum*.

BEGONIA ELATIOR HYBRIDS

Single or double flowers mainly red, pink, yellow, orange and white, all seasons, especially winter.

Temperature: winter minimum 13–21°C (55–70°F) while growing.
Humidity: high humidity is beneficial.
Position: good light, not direct summer sun. Best possible light in winter.
Watering and feeding: water freely while in flower. Feed with weak fertilizer while in bud and flowering.
Care: deadhead regularly. Discard after flowering.
Propagation: propagate from leaf or tip cuttings.

BEGONIA FOLIAGE

Foliage begonias are attractive all year. Several species, all compact, with hairy or puckered leaves in brightly variegated colours.

Temperature: winter minimum 16°C (60°F).
Humidity: require high humidity, but avoid spraying leaves.
Position: good light, not direct sun.
Watering and feeding: water freely from spring to autumn, sparingly in winter.
Care: repot annually in spring.
Propagation: division; leaf cuttings.

25

BILLBERGIA NUTANS

Bromeliad with yellow-and-green, blue-edged flowers with pink bracts, in spring.

Temperature: winter minimum 13°C (55°F).
Humidity: tolerates dry air if necessary.
Position: good light, not direct sun.
Watering and feeding: water freely from spring to autumn, sparingly in winter. In summer pour some water into the leaf rosettes. Feed from spring to autumn.
Care: allow offsets around base to grow into a large clump – they will soon flower. Repot when clump fills the pot.
Propagation: offsets (separate when new shoots are half as tall as parent plant).

BROWALLIA SPECIOSA

Bushy herbaceous plant with blue, purple or white flowers. Many varieties. Regular sowing ensures year-round colour.

Temperature: 10–15°C (50–59°F) for longer flowering.
Humidity: undemanding, but mist leaves occasionally.
Position: good light. Tolerates some direct sun, but not through glass at hottest part of the day.
Watering and feeding: water freely at all times. Feed regularly.
Care: grow one plant in a 10 cm (4 in) pot, or three in a 15 cm (6 in) pot. Pinch out growing tips for bushiness. Deadhead regularly. Discard plant after flowering.
Propagation: seed, in late winter or early spring.

CAMPANULA ISOPHYLLA

Trailing stems with soft blue, star-like flowers in mid and late summer.

Temperature: winter minimum 7°C (45°F) for longer flowering.
Humidity: undemanding, but mist leaves occasionally.
Position: good light, avoid direct summer sun.
Watering and feeding: water freely from spring to autumn, sparingly in winter. Feed regularly.
Care: deadhead regularly. Cut stems back to 5–7.5 cm (2–3 in) at end of growing season.
Propagation: seed; or can take cuttings.

CELOSIA CRISTATA

Deeply ruffled flowers in red, yellow, orange and pink, in summer and early autumn. The Plumosa group has feathery flower plumes.

Temperature: 10–15°C (50–59°F) if possible.

Humidity: moderate humidity.

Position: good light, avoid direct summer sun through glass.

Watering and feeding: water moderately; vulnerable to under- and overwatering. Feed regularly but cautiously – too much leads to poor flowers.

Care: raise in greenhouse or buy as young plants. Discard after flowering.

Propagation: seed.

CEROPEGIA WOODII

Succulent trailer with heart-shaped leaves, with silver mottling.

Temperature: winter minimum 10°C (50°F).

Humidity: tolerates dry air.

Position: good light, tolerates full sun and partial shade.

Watering and feeding: water sparingly at all times. Feed regularly with weak fertilizer in summer.

Care: shorten bare spindly stems in spring.

Propagation: Seed; layering; stem tuber cuttings.

CHAMAEDOREA ELEGANS

Compact palm with arching leaves growing from base, and tiny yellow ball flowers.

Temperature: winter 12–15°C (53–59°F).

Humidity: mist occasionally, even in winter if the room is centrally heated.

Position: good light, avoid direct summer sun.

Watering and feeding: water generously from spring to autumn, keep just moist in winter. Feed regularly in spring and summer with weak fertilizer.

Care: repot when roots grow through bottom of pot.

Propagation: seed; division.

Chlorophytum Comosum 'Vittatum'

Arching, linear white-and-green variegated leaves, 30–60 cm (12–24 in) long. Long stalks bear small white flowers and leaf plantlets.

Temperature: winter minimum 7°C (45°F).
Humidity: mist leaves occasionally.
Position: good light, not direct sun.
Watering and feeding: water generously spring to autumn, sparingly in winter. Feed regularly from spring to autumn.
Care: repot young plants each spring, mature ones when roots push the plant out of pot.
Propagation: stem plantlets; division.

Chrysanthemum Year-round

Compact plants for year-round colour, in red, pink, purple, yellow and white.

Temperature: 10–15°C (50–59°F). Tolerates a warm room, but flowers will be shorter-lived.
Humidity: undemanding; mist leaves from time to time.
Position: undemanding.
Watering and feeding: keep moist.
Care: deadhead regularly. Discard after flowering or transfer to garden.
Propagation: None.

Cissus Rhombifolia

Vigorous climber with dark green leaves.

Temperature: winter 7–13°C (45–55°F).
Humidity: undemanding, but mist leaves occasionally, especially in summer.
Position: good light, avoid direct summer sun.
Watering and feeding: water generously from spring to autumn, but sparingly in winter.
Care: pinch out growing tips on young plants; tie new shoots to the support. Thin overcrowded shoots in spring.
Propagation: cuttings.

x *Citrofortunella Microcarpa*

Glossy, dark green evergreen plant up to 1.2 m (4 ft) high. Clusters of fragrant white flowers, usually in summer, followed by miniature orange fruits.

Temperature: winter minimum 10°C (50°F).

Humidity: undemanding, but mist leaves occasionally.

Position: good light, avoid direct summer sun through glass.

Watering and feeding: water freely in summer, sparingly in winter. Feed regularly in summer, perhaps including magnesium and iron.

Care: pollinate flowers using cotton wool.

Propagation: cuttings.

Clivia Miniata

Evergreen perennial with strap-shaped leaves. Large flower head of orange or yellow funnel-shaped flowers, in early spring.

Temperature: winter minimum 10°C (50°F). Avoid warm winter temperatures.

Humidity: undemanding; mist leaves occasionally.

Position: good light, avoid direct summer sun.

Watering and feeding: water moderately from spring to autumn, sparingly in winter until flower stalk is 15 cm (6 in). Feed from flowering to early autumn.

Care: sponge leaves occasionally. Repot when roots push plant from pot, after flowering. Winter in unheated room.

Propagation: division (after flowering).

Cocos Nucifera

Tall and slow-growing palm with visible coconut. Grows to 3 m (10 ft) indoors.

Temperature: winter minimum 18°C (64°F).

Humidity: high humidity.

Position: good light, some full sun, but avoid direct sun through glass during hottest part of day.

Watering and feeding: water freely in summer, moderately in winter. Feed with weak fertilizer in summer.

Care: sponge leaves occasionally; never use leaf shine. Repot young plants in the spring.

Propagation: seed (difficult at home, can be done by a professional plantsman).

CODIAEUM VARIEGATUM PICTUM

Many varieties with colourful or variegated, glossy, evergreen leaves, many colours.

Temperature: winter minimum 16°C (60°F).
Humidity: high humidity. Mist leaves regularly.
Position: good light, avoid direct summer sun.
Watering and feeding: water generously from spring to autumn, sparingly in winter. Feed regularly in spring and summer.
Care: avoid cold draughts. Repot when outgrown pot.
Propagation: cuttings.

COLCHICUM AUTUMNALE

Corms producing large crocus-shaped, pink flowers in early autumn.
Temperature: undemanding and hardy.
Humidity: undemanding.

Position: light windowsill, preferably out of strong direct sunlight.
Watering and feeding: none required.
Care: place dry corms in saucer of sand or tray of dry pebbles, set in light position and leave to flower. After flowering plant in garden in light shade.
Propagation: buy new corms.

COLEUS BLUMEI HYBRIDS

Perennial sub-shrubs treated as annuals.
Variegated leaves in a range of pattern and colour – reds, yellows and greens.
Temperature: winter minimum 10°C (50°F).
Humidity: high humidity. Mist leaves frequently.
Position: good light, avoid direct summer sun.
Watering and feeding: water freely from spring to autumn, keep roots just moist in winter. Use soft water. Feed from spring to autumn.
Care: pinch out growing tips of young plants, several times for really bushy plants. Cut back hard old overwintered plants and repot in spring. If grown from seed, retain most appealing and discard the rest.
Propagation: seed in spring; stem cuttings in spring or summer.

COLUMNEA

Trailing evergreen perennials with red or orange-red flowers, winter or early spring.

Temperature: winter minimum 13°C (55°F).
Humidity: high humidity. Mist regularly.
Position: good light, but avoid direct summer sun.
Watering and feeding: water freely from spring to autumn, sparingly in winter. Feed regularly in spring and summer.
Care: shorten stems after flowering. Repot every second or third year, in humus-rich, fibrous potting mixture.
Propagation: cuttings.

CROCUS

Mainly spring-flowering corms. Plant in autumn for late winter to early spring colour.
Temperature: keep cool.
Humidity: undemanding.
Position: good light indoors.

Watering and feeding: water cautiously.
Care: leave in garden until mid-winter, but protect from excessive freezing and waterlogging. Maintain cool conditions in house until at least a third of developing flower bud is visible. After flowering plant in garden.
Propagation: new corms; offset corms; and seed.

CYCLAMEN

Tuber for autumn to spring colour, in pinks, red, purples, salmon and white.

Temperature: 10–15°C (50–59°F) in winter.
Humidity: moderate humidity. Stand pot on tray of wet pebbles. Mist leaves only.
Position: Good light, not direct sun.
Watering and feeding: water freely while actively growing, gradually reduce after flowering. Feed regularly during active growing and flowering periods.
Care: deadhead regularly, removing entire stalk. When leaves have died, keep cool (perhaps outside) and almost dry until mid-summer. Start watering, repot if necessary (burying tuber to half its depth) and bring indoors if outside.
Propagation: seed.

31

CYPERUS

Rush-like plants, with leaves radiating from stiff stalks. Tolerates overwatering.
Temperature: winter minimum 7°C (45°F).
Humidity: mist regularly.
Position: good light, avoid direct summer sun.
Watering and feeding: water

freely at all times, keeping roots moist. Feed from mid-spring to early autumn.
Care: cut off yellowing stems. Repot in spring.
Propagation: division.

DIEFFENBACHIA MACULATA

Bold oval leaves with ivory or cream markings. Poisonous or irritant sap.
Temperature: winter minimum 16°C (60°F).

Humidity: mist leaves regularly.
Position: partial shade and good light, avoid direct summer sun.
Watering and feeding: water freely from spring to autumn, sparingly in winter. Feed regularly in spring and summer.
Care: wash leaves occasionally. Repot each spring.
Propagation: cane or stem cuttings.

DIZYGOTHECA ELEGANTISSIMA

Graceful evergreen with dark green, almost black, elongated, serrated leaves. Grows up to 1.2 m (4 ft) tall.
Temperature: winter minimum 13°C (55°F).

Humidity: mist regularly.
Position: good light, avoid direct summer sun at hottest part of day.
Watering and feeding: water moderately from spring to autumn, sparingly in winter.
Care: repot every second spring.
Propagation: seed or air layering in spring; tip cuttings in summer.

DRACAENA

Tough, palm-like foliage plants with striking variegation and bold outline.

Temperature: winter minimum 13°C (55°F).
Humidity: mist leaves regularly.
Position: good light, not direct sun.
Watering and feeding: water freely from spring to autumn, sparingly in winter. Never let roots dry out. Feed regularly in spring and summer.
Care: sponge leaves occasionally. Repot in spring if necessary.
Propagation: tip cuttings; air layering; cane cuttings.

ECHEVERIA

Rosette-forming succulents grown for shape and bluish-grey colouring. Yellow, pink or red flowers, from spring through to mid-summer.
Temperature: winter 5–10°C (41–50°F).
Humidity: tolerates dry air.
Position: best possible light. Will tolerate full sun.

Watering and feeding: water moderately from spring to autumn, practically dry in winter. Feed with weak fertilizer in spring and summer.
Care: avoid getting water on leaves. Can use winter-fallen tips as cuttings.
Propagation: tip cuttings; leaf cuttings; offsets; seed.

ECHINOCACTUS GRUSONII

Slow-growing spherical cactus, more cylindrical with age.
Temperature: winter 5–10°C (41–50°F).

Humidity: tolerates dry air.
Position: best possible light. Tolerates full sun.
Watering and feeding: water moderately from spring to autumn, practically dry in winter. Feed with weak fertilizer in spring and summer.
Care: repot only as necessary, using cactus mixture.
Propagation: seed.

Epipremnum Aureum

Climber or trailer with heart-shaped glossy leaves, blotched or streaked with yellow.

Temperature: winter minimum 13°C (55°F).
Humidity: undemanding, but benefits from occasional misting.
Position: good light, not direct sun.
Watering and feeding: water freely from spring to autumn, sparingly in winter. Feed in spring and summer.
Care: repot in spring if necessary. To keep plant compact, shorten long shoots.
Propagation: leaf bud cuttings; stem tip cuttings; layering.

Erica

Two species provide indoor winter colour.
E. gracilis: white-tipped, pink urn-shaped flowers;
E. hyemalis white, pink or reddish bell-shaped flowers.

Temperature: 5–13°C (41–55°F) when flowering.
Humidity: mist leaves regularly.
Position: good light. Benefits from winter sun.
Watering and feeding: water freely at all times. Never allow roots to dry out. Soft water if possible.
Care: buy when in flower, then discard.
Propagation: cuttings.

Eustoma Grandiflorum

Short-term, compact plant with blue, pink and white poppy flowers, in summer.

Temperature: winter minimum 7°C (45°F).
Humidity: Mist occasionally.
Position: good light, but avoid direct summer sun.
Watering and feeding: water with care. Do not overwater but keep compost moist. Feed regularly once nutrients in potting soil are depleted.
Care: discard when flowering finished.
Propagation: seeds.

EXACUM AFFINE

Masses of small, pale purple or white flowers, from mid-summer to late autumn.

Temperature: 10–21°C (50–70°F).

Humidity: mist leaves regularly.

Position: good light, avoid direct summer sun.

Watering and feeding: water freely. Feed regularly once nutrients in potting soil are depleted.

Care: deadhead regularly. Discard after flowering.

Propagation: seed.

x *FATSHEDERA LIZEI*

Tall growing foliage plant with shiny, five-fingered leaves. Attractive variegations.

Temperature: winter minimum 3°C (37°F).

Humidity: undemanding in a cool position, but mist occasionally in a warm room.

Position: good light, avoid direct summer sun. Best possible light in winter.

Watering and feeding: water freely from spring to autumn, sparingly in winter. Tepid water if possible. Feed in spring and summer.

Care: repot each spring. Provide support to grow tall, or pinch growing tips each spring for bushy plant.

Propagation: cuttings.

FATSIA JAPONICA

Large, deeply lobed, glossy dark green leaves. Also variegated varieties.

Temperature: winter minimum 3°C (37°F), 13°C (55°F) for variegated types. Keep below 21°C (70°F) if possible.

Humidity: moderate humidity.

Position: good light, avoid direct summer sun. Tolerates shade.

Watering and feeding: water freely from spring to autumn, sparingly in winter. Never let roots dry out. Feed in spring and summer.

Care: sponge leaves monthly. Repot in spring if necessary.

Propagation: cuttings; air layering; seed.

Ficus Benjamina

Pendulous shoots with green leaves, up to 2.4 m (8 ft) indoors, useful for focal plant. 'Starlight': variegated leaves.
Temperature: winter minimum 13°C (55°F).
Humidity: mist the leaves occasionally.

Position: good light, avoid direct summer sun during hottest part of day.
Watering and feeding: water freely from spring to autumn, sparingly in winter, using tepid water. Feed in spring and summer.
Care: repot young plants every second year.
Propagation: cuttings; air layering.

Fittonia Verschaffeltii

Creeping plant with pink-veined, olive-green leaves, about 5 cm (2 in) long.

Temperature: winter minimum 16°C (60°F).
Humidity: high humidity.

Position: partial shade, not direct sun.
Watering and feeding: water freely from spring to autumn, sparingly in winter. Tepid water if possible. Feed from spring to autumn with weak fertilizer.
Care: pinch back straggly shoots. Repot each spring. Does best in a bottle garden.
Propagation: division; cuttings; pot up where rooted.

Fuchsia Hybrids

Compact deciduous shrubs grown for their bell-shaped flowers with flared "skirts", in a range of colours. Grows to 45–60 cm (18–24 in).

Temperature: winter 10–16°C (50–60°F).
Humidity: mist leaves occasionally.
Position: good light, not direct summer sun.
Watering and feeding: water freely from spring to autumn while plant is growing vigorously, otherwise sparingly, and very sparingly in winter if plants are dormant. Feed from late spring through summer.
Care: shorten old shoots just before or as new growth starts; pruning can be severe. Repot every second or third year in humus-rich, fibrous potting mixture.
Propagation: cuttings.

GARDENIA JASMINOIDES

Glossy evergreen shrub. Large, fragrant, white flowers, in summer. 45 cm (18 in) houseplant or 1.5 m (5 ft) in conservatory.

Temperature: winter minimum 16°C (60°F).
Humidity: mist leaves regularly.
Position: good light, but avoid direct summer sun during hottest part of day.
Watering and feeding: water freely from spring to autumn, sparingly in winter, never let roots become dry. Soft water if possible. Feed from spring to autumn.
Care: avoid widely fluctuating temperatures when buds forming. Repot every second or third year with ericaceous potting soil.
Propagation: cuttings.

HEDERA

Self-clinging climbers or trailers, many varieties, including variegated ones.
H. canariensis: large lobed leaves.
H. helix: small leaves.

Temperature: cool but frost-free.
Humidity: mist leaves occasionally, regularly in summer.
Position: good light or some shade, avoid direct summer sun.
Watering and feeding: water freely in warm weather, moderately in cool temperatures, never let roots become dry. Soft water if possible. Feed regularly from spring to autumn.
Care: repot each spring, unless in a large pot. Pinch out growing tips periodically for a bushy plant.
Propagation: cuttings.

HIBISCUS ROSA-SINENSIS

Large-flowered evergreen in many colours, spring to autumn.
Up to 75 cm (2½ ft). 'Cooperi': variegated foliage and red flowers.
Temperature: winter minimum 13°C (55°F).
Humidity: mist leaves occasionally.
Position: good light, avoid direct summer sun during hottest part of day.
Watering and feeding: water freely from spring to autumn, sparingly in winter, but never allow roots to dry out. Feed regularly in summer.
Care: deadhead regularly. Shorten long shoots after flowering or in late winter. Once buds form do not turn plant. Repot each spring.
Propagation: cuttings; seed.

HOWEA BELMOREANA

Evergreen palms with thin green stems and arching, pinnate foliage. Can grow to ceiling height.

Temperature: winter minimum 16°C (60°F).

Humidity: mist leaves regularly.

Position: good light, avoid direct summer sun during hottest part of day.

Watering and feeding: water moderately in summer, sparingly in winter. Keep soil just moist. Feed in summer.

Care: sponge leaves occasionally. Don't use leaf shine.

Propagation: seed (difficult).

HOYA BELLA

Fleshy-leaved evergreen climber or trailer. Pendulous clusters of fragrant, white star-shaped flowers, through summer.

Temperature: winter minimum of 18°C (64°F).

Humidity: mist leaves regularly, except when in bloom.

Position: good light, avoid summer sun through glass during hottest part of day.

Watering and feeding: water freely from spring to autumn, sparingly in winter, but never allow roots to dry out. Feed sparingly when in flower.

Care: provide support if grown as climber. Repot only when necessary and never once flower buds formed.

Propagation: semi-ripe cuttings; also eye cuttings.

HYACINTHUS ORIENTALIS

Indoor bulbs for winter and early spring colour and fragrance, in many colours.

Temperature: hardy. Keep as cool as possible unless advancing flowering.

Humidity: undemanding.

Position: good light once buds begin to show colour. Anywhere once in full flower.

Watering and feeding: Ensure roots do not dry out. Feed only if planting bulbs in garden.

Care: discard after flowering, or plant in garden.

Propagation: buy fresh bulbs each year.

HYDRANGEA MACROPHYLLA

Deciduous shrubs with ball-shaped flower heads in blue, pink or white, usually in spring, but sometimes at other times.

Temperature: winter minimum 7°C (45°F). Move to warm bright position in mid-winter, when you can increase watering.
Humidity: mist occasionally.
Position: good light or light shade. Avoid direct summer sun.
Watering and feeding: water freely from spring to autumn, sparingly in early winter. Soft water if possible. Feed regularly during active growth.
Care: flower colour is affected by the type of potting soil: use ericaceous for blue flowers. Never allow roots to dry out during growing season. Stand outside after flowering. Repot every second or third year with ericaceous potting soil.
Propagation: semi-ripe cuttings.

HYPOESTES PHYLLOSTACHYA

Evergreen with pointed oval leaves covered with red or pink spots or blotches.
Temperature: winter minimum 13°C (55°F).
Humidity: mist leaves regularly.

Position: good light, avoid direct summer sun during hottest part of day.
Watering and feeding: water freely from spring to autumn, sparingly in winter, soil just moist. Feed regularly in summer; spindly growth results from overfeeding.

Care: pinch out leaf tips and cut back straggly shoots. Pinch out flowers – these spoil compact shape.
Propagation: cuttings; seed.

IMPATIENS HYBRIDS

Compact plants with masses of flat flowers in red, orange, pink or white, year-round.

Temperature: winter minimum 13°C (55°F), or 16°C (60°F) if flowering.
Humidity: mist leaves occasionally, avoiding flowers.
Position: good light, avoid direct summer sun.
Watering and feeding: water freely from spring to autumn, sparingly in winter.
Care: pinch out tips of young plants. Cut back lanky old plants, or discard.
Propagation: seed; cuttings.

JASMINUM

Woody climbers with very fragrant flowers, suitable for conservatory, usually deciduous.

J. officinale: white summer flowers. *J. polyanthum*: white winter flowers.

Temperature: winter minimum 7°C (45°F).
Humidity: mist leaves regularly.
Position: good light with some direct sun.
Watering and feeding: water freely from spring to autumn, in winter keep soil barely moist. Feed regularly during active growth.
Care: large pot with support. Prune to contain size if necessary. Avoid high winter temperatures.
Propagation: cuttings.

JUSTICIA BRANDEGEEANA

Evergreen grown for long-lasting reddish-brown bracts, available all year. Rarely reaches its potential 90 cm (3 ft).

Temperature: winter 10–16°C (50–60°F).
Humidity: mist occasionally.
Position: good light with some direct sun, but not through glass in summer.
Watering and feeding: water freely from spring to autumn, sparingly in winter. Feed regularly from spring to autumn.
Care: repot each spring, and prune back shoots by one-third.
Propagation: cuttings.

KALANCHOE BLOSSFELDIANA

Fleshy-leaved succulent. Flowers in various colours, year-round.

Temperature: winter minimum 10°C (50°F).
Humidity: tolerates dry air.
Position: good light with some direct sun, but avoid direct summer sun during hottest part of day.
Watering and feeding: water freely from spring to autumn, sparingly in winter. Feed regularly from spring to autumn.
Care: discard after flowering.
Propagation: cuttings; seed.

LILIUM HYBRIDS

Indoor bulbs for spring colour and fragrance, in many colours, usually mottled.

Temperature: 3–10°C (37–50°F), avoid high temperatures.
Humidity: mist occasionally.
Position: good light, but avoid direct summer sun.
Watering and feeding: keep soil moist during active growth. Feed regularly.
Care: pot bulb in autumn or winter when bought, with at least 5 cm (2 in) soil beneath and 10 cm (4 in) above. Keep in cool place with soil just moist, ensuring good light once shoots appear. Move in to house when buds show colour. Plant in garden after flowering.
Propagation: buy fresh bulbs each year.

LITHOPS

Prostrate succulents with pairs of fused swollen leaves resembling pebbles.

Temperature: winter minimum 7°C (45°F).
Humidity: tolerates dry air.
Position: good light with plenty of sun.
Watering and feeding: water moderately in summer. Keep dry in winter. Recommence when old leaves split to reveal new ones. Only feed after many years in same pot, with cactus fertilizer.
Care: repot only when the pot filled with leaves.
Propagation: seed.

MARANTA LEUCONEURA ERYTHRONEURA

Squat foliage plants with strikingly marked round oval leaves.

Temperature: winter minimum 10°C (50°F).
Humidity: high humidity. Mist the leaves regularly.
Position: good light, avoid direct summer sun. Best possible light in winter.
Watering and feeding: water freely from spring to summer. Soft water if possible. Feed regularly in summer.
Care: repot every second spring.
Propagation: division.

MONSTERA DELICIOSA

Thick-stemmed climber with very large leaves, perforated with age. Can grow to reach the ceiling.

Temperature: winter minimum 10°C (50°F).
Humidity: mist leaves regularly.
Position: good light or shade, not direct sun. Best possible light in winter.
Watering and feeding: water freely from spring to autumn, sparingly in winter. Feed regularly in summer.
Care: provide support. Lightly sponge leaves occasionally.
Propagation: cuttings; air layering.

NARCISSUS HYBRIDS

Bulbs for late winter and early spring colour. White, fragrant 'Paperwhite' and yellow 'Soleil d'Or' are suitable for forcing.

Temperature: 15–21°C (59–70°F).
Humidity: undemanding.
Position: good light.
Watering and feeding: water moderately while bulbs growing.
Care: grow in pots or in bowls of water supported by pebbles, keeping base of bulb above water.
Propagation: buy fresh bulbs each year.

NEPHROLEPSIS EXALTATA

Evergreen fern forming a dense clump of pinnate leaves, varying according to the variety.

Temperature: winter minimum 18°C (64°F).
Humidity: mist leaves regularly.
Position: partial shade, not direct sun.
Watering and feeding: water freely in summer, cautiously in winter, keeping roots moist without being wet. Use soft water if possible.
Care: repot in spring if becomes too large for pot. Avoid draughts.
Propagation: plantlets; spores (species only).

NERTERA GRANADENSIS

Mound-forming, creeping perennial grown for bright orange berries, in autumn.

Temperature: winter minimum 7°C (45°F).
Humidity: mist leaves occasionally.
Position: good light, with some direct sun.
Watering and feeding: water freely from spring to autumn, sparingly in winter. Never allow roots to dry out completely.
Care: can leave outdoors all summer until berries form. Discard after berries finished.
Propagation: division; seed.

OPUNTIA

Branching cacti, some cylindrical, some with flat pads. Red or yellow flowers.
Temperature: winter minimum 7°C (45°F).
Humidity: tolerates dry air as it is a desert plant.

Position: Best possible light, benefits from direct sun.
Watering and feeding: water moderately from spring to autumn, very sparingly in winter. Feed in summer with weak fertilizer or cactus food.
Care: repot in spring if necessary. Flat pad types do well in ordinary loam-based potting soil, others prefer cactus mixture.
Propagation: cuttings or detach pads; seed.

PARRODIA

Rounded to cylindrical cacti with bristly spines. Yellow flowers in spring.

Temperature: winter 7–12°C (45–53°F).
Humidity: tolerates dry air as it is a desert plant.
Position: Best possible light, benefits from full sun.
Watering and feeding: water moderately from spring to autumn, leave practically dry in winter. Use soft water if possible. Feed in summer with weak fertilizer or cactus food.
Care: Plants are slow-growing, but if they need repotting use a special cactus mixture if possible.
Propagation: seed.

PELARGONIUM, REGAL OR MARTHA WASHINGTON

Scalloped leaves and showy, often bicoloured blooms from early spring to mid-summer.

Temperature: winter minimum 7°C (45°F).

Humidity: tolerates dry air.

Position: good light with some sun. Tolerates full sun.

Watering and feeding: water moderately between spring and autumn. Feed regularly from spring to autumn.

Care: can be kept in leaf if given sufficient warmth. Repot in spring if necessary. Deadhead regularly. Shorten long shoots in autumn. Pinch out growing tip for bushy growth.

Propagation: cuttings; seed.

PELLAEA

Ferns with feathery fronds. Tolerate dry conditions, humidity improves growth.

Temperature: winter 13–16°C (55–60°F).

Humidity: mist leaves occasionally.

Position: good light, not direct sun.

Watering and feeding: water moderately at all times, with care. Feed with weak fertilizer in summer.

Care: if repotting, use shallow container or hanging basket.

Propagation: division; spores.

PEPEROMIA

Undemanding compact, slow-growing foliage plants with wide variety of leaf shapes, colouring and size.

Temperature: winter minimum 10°C (50°F).

Humidity: mist leaves occasionally with warm water, not in winter.

Position: semi-shade or good light, avoid direct summer sun.

Watering and feeding: water moderately from spring to autumn, cautiously in winter. Soft water if possible. Feed from spring to autumn.

Care: repot only when necessary to slightly larger pot, in spring, with peat-based mix.

Propagation: cuttings; leaf cuttings.

PHILODENDRON SCANDENS

Climber or trailer with heart-shaped, glossy green leaves. Can reach ceiling.
Temperature: winter minimum 13°C (55°F).
Humidity: mist leaves regularly.
Position: good light, avoid direct summer sun. Tolerates low light levels well.

Watering and feeding: water freely from spring to autumn. Soft water if possible. Feed from spring to autumn; to limit growth avoid nitrogen feeds.
Care: provide suitable support.
Propagation: cuttings; air layering.

PHOENIX CANARIENSIS

Palm with feathery fronds, stiff at first, arching later.

Temperature: winter minimum 7°C (45°F).
Humidity: tolerates dry air.
Position: good light, especially direct sun.
Watering and feeding: water moderately from spring to autumn, sparingly in winter. Feed regularly from spring to autumn.
Care: repot only when becomes pot-bound, in deep container.
Propagation: seed.

PILEA

Bushy or trailing foliage plants. Many textured and with silver or bronze markings.

Temperature: winter minimum 10°C (50°F).
Humidity: mist leaves regularly.
Position: good light or partial shade, avoid direct summer sun.
Watering and feeding: water freely while in active growth. Feed regularly from spring to autumn.
Care: pinch out growing tips of young plants and again a month or two later. Repot in spring.
Propagation: cuttings.

PRIMULA OBCONICA

Rounded, fragrant flowers, in winter and spring. Leaves can cause allergic reaction.

Temperature: winter minimum 13°C (55°F).
Humidity: mist leaves occasionally.
Position: good light, not direct sun.
Watering and feeding: water moderately from autumn to spring, sparingly in summer. Feed regularly during flowering with weak fertilizer.
Care: keep cool during summer.
Propagation: seed.

PTERIS

Ferns with deeply divided fronds. Several variegated varieties.
Temperature: winter minimum: 13°C (55°F) for pale green forms; 16°C (60°F) for variegated ones.
Humidity: mist leaves regularly.
Position: good

light, not direct sun. Plain green forms will tolerate poorer light than variegated varieties.
Watering and feeding: water freely from spring to autumn, sparingly in winter. Soft water if possible. Feed regularly with weak fertilizer from spring to autumn.
Care: never allow roots to become dry.
Propagation: division; spores.

RADERMACHERA SINICA

Vigorous, evergreen, bushy foliage plant with individual leaflets, about 60 cm (24 in) tall.

Temperature: winter minimum 13°C (55°F).
Humidity: undemanding.
Position: good light, avoid direct summer sun during hottest part of day.
Watering and feeding: water freely from spring to autumn, moderately in winter.
Care: Pinch out growing tips of young plants.
Propagation: cuttings.

REBUTIA

Rounded or oval cacti with bristly spines. Flowers in spring or early summer.

Temperature: winter minimum 5°C (41°F).
Humidity: tolerates dry air, but appreciates humid atmosphere in spring and summer.
Position: good light, full sun.
Watering and feeding: water moderately from spring to autumn, almost dry in winter. Feed in summer with cactus food.
Care: repot in spring if necessary, using cactus mixture.
Propagation: cuttings from offshoots; seed.

RHODODENDRON

R. x *obtusum* (range of colours) and R. *simsii* (pinks and reds) are good for winter and spring colour. Known as azaleas.

Temperature: winter 10–16°C (50–60°F).
Humidity: mist leaves regularly.

Position: good light, not direct sun.
Watering and feeding: water freely at all times, using soft water if possible. Feed regularly in summer.
Care: repot in ericaceous mixture one month after flowering. Place in garden in sheltered shady spot after all danger of frost is past. Keep watered and fed. R. *simsii* must be brought indoors in early autumn.
Propagation: cuttings.

ROSA, MINIATURE HYBRIDS

Miniature bushes or standards make short-term houseplants in various colours.

Temperature: frost hardy. 10–21°C (50–70°F) when plants growing actively.
Humidity: undemanding, but advisable to mist occasionally.
Position: best possible light. Tolerates full sun.
Watering and feeding: water freely from spring to autumn, while in leaf. Feed regularly in summer.
Care: place outdoors when not in flower. Repot in autumn if necessary. Prune in spring. Bring indoors in late spring, or as soon as flowering starts.
Propagation: cuttings.

47

SAINTPAULIA

Rosette-forming, hairy-leaved perennials with large colour range. Long-flowering with appropriate light intensities.

Temperature: winter minimum 16°C (60°F).
Humidity: high humidity, stand on tray of wet pebbles; misting is unsuitable.
Position: good light, avoid direct summer sun during hottest part of day. Artificial light at least 5,000 lux.
Watering and feeding: water freely from spring to autumn, moderately in winter, allowing surface to dry out a little. Soft water if possible. Don't wet leaves. Feed during active growth, but stop if lots of leaves and few flowers.
Care: will continue flowering with supplemental light, but needs at least one month's rest; lower temperature to minimum, reduce watering and shorten day length. Place the plant in good light to restart growth.
Propagation: leaf cuttings; seed.

SANSEVIERIA TRIFASCIATA 'LAURENTII'

Tough, fleshy, sword-like leaves, dull green with paler cross-banding and yellow edges.

Temperature: winter minimum 10°C (50°F).
Humidity: tolerates dry air.
Position: bright, indirect light, but it tolerates direct sun and some shade.
Watering and feeding: water moderately from spring to autumn, very sparingly in winter. Always allow the soil to dry out slightly before watering. Feed regularly in summer.
Care: repotting is seldom required.
Propagation: division.

SAXIFRAGA STOLONIFERA

Trailing alpine with rounded, broadly toothed leaves, olive green with veining.

Temperature: winter minimum 7°C (45°F).
Humidity: mist occasionally.
Position: good light, not direct sun.
Watering and feeding: water freely from spring to autumn, sparingly in winter. Feed regularly in summer.
Care: trim off long runners if untidy.
Propagation: plantlets (peg down in pots).

SCHEFFLERA ARBORICOLA 'AUREA'

Erect, branched, variegated evergreen with oval leaflets radiating from each leaf stalk.

Temperature: winter minimum of 13°C (55°F).
Humidity: mist regularly.
Position: good light, avoid direct sun.
Watering and feeding: water freely from spring to autumn, sparingly in winter. Feed regularly in summer.
Care: either train as upright, unbranching plant by staking, or remove growing tip to make bushy. Repot annually in spring.

SEDUM

Small, fleshy, branching succulents, some with white, pink or yellow flowers.
Temperature: winter minimum 5°C (41°F).
Humidity: tolerates dry air.

Position: best possible light.
Watering and feeding: water sparingly from spring to autumn, keep nearly dry during winter.
Care: repot in spring, using free-draining potting soil such as cactus mixture.
Propagation: leaf cuttings (for large fleshy leaves); stem cuttings.

SINNINGIA SPECIOSA

Tuberous perennials with large, hairy leaves and bell-shaped flowers in various colours, in summer. It is often sold as *gloxinia*.

Temperature: minimum 16°C (60°F) during growing season.
Humidity: mist around plant regularly, but avoid wetting leaves or flowers. Provide as much humidity as possible.
Position: good light, not direct sun.
Watering and feeding: water freely once tubers have rooted well. Decrease at end of growing season. Feed regularly in the summer months.
Care: store tubers in the pot in frost-free place, ideally at 10°C (50°F). Repot in the spring.
Propagation: leaf cuttings; seed.

SOLANUM CAPSICASTRUM

Sub-shrubs grown for their autumn to winter fruit (green turning red). Poisonous fruit.

Temperature: winter 10–16°C (50–60°F).
Humidity: mist leaves regularly.
Position: best possible light. Tolerates some direct sun.
Watering and feeding: water freely through growing period. Feed regularly in summer.
Care: buy in fruit or raise in greenhouse until fruit formed.
Propagation: seed; cuttings.

SOLEIROLIA SOLEIROLII

Compact, mounded plant, with tiny leaves, 5 cm (2 in) high. Silver and gold varieties.

Temperature: frost hardy, but 7°C (45°F) is ideal.
Humidity: mist regularly.
Position: good light, not direct sun.
Watering and feeding: water freely.
Care: repot in spring in low, wide container.
Propagation: division.

SPARRMANNIA AFRICANA

Tall and fast-growing ever-green with pale green, downy leaves. White spring flowers.

Temperature: winter minimum 7°C (45°F).
Humidity: mist occasionally.
Position: good light, but not direct summer sun during the hottest part of the day.
Watering and feeding: water freely from spring through to autumn, sparingly in the winter. Feed regularly in spring and summer.
Care: cut back stems after flowering. When repotting, cut back to 30 cm (12 in) if necessary. Young plants may need repotting seveal times a year to accommodate its fast growth. Pinch out growing tips of young plants for a bushy shape.
Propagation: cuttings.

STEPHANOTIS FLORIBUNDA

Climber with glossy, oval leaves. Clusters of fragrant white flowers in summer.

Temperature: winter 13–16°C (55–60°F).
Humidity: mist occasionally.
Position: good light, avoid direct summer sun during hottest part of day.
Watering and feeding: water freely from spring to autumn, sparingly in winter. Feed regularly in summer, in moderation if plant is large.
Care: train to a support. Shorten overlong shoots and cut out overcrowded stems in spring.
Propagation: cuttings.

STREPTOCARPUS HYBRIDS

Perennial with horizontal, stemless leaves and large trumpet-shaped flowers in pink, red and blue, late spring through summer. Leaf sap can cause an irritating rash.

Temperature: winter minimum 13°C (55°F).
Humidity: lightly mist leaves occasionally.
Position: good light, avoid direct summer sun.
Watering and feeding: water freely from spring to autumn, sparingly in winter. Feed regularly in summer.
Care: benefits from dormant winter season, with soil only slightly moist and temperature close to winter minimum. Repot early spring.
Propagation: leaf cuttings; seed.

SYNGONIUM PODOPHYLLUM

Evergreen climber with foot-shaped leaves, arrow-shaped on young plants. Variegated varieties. Will grow to 1.8 m (6 ft).

Temperature: winter minimum 16°C (60°F).
Humidity: mist leaves regularly.
Position: good light, not direct sun. Tolerates low light levels.
Watering and feeding: water freely from spring to autumn, sparingly in winter but do not allow it to dry out completely. Feed regularly in spring and summer.
Care: to retain juvenile leaves, cut off climbing stems at the base. Repot the plant every second spring.
Propagation: cuttings; air layering.

TILLANDSIA CYNEA

Rosette of narrow, striped grass-like leaves. Summer flower spike has pink or red bract and purple-blue flowers.

Temperature: winter minimum 18°C (64°F).
Humidity: mist regularly.
Position: good light, not direct summer sun.
Watering and feeding: water freely from spring to autumn, sparingly in winter. Soft water if possible. Apply weak fertilizer to leaves, using mister, or to soil.
Care: can pot in spring.
Propagation: offsets.

TOLMIEA MENZIESII

Bright green foliage plant with heart-shaped leaves. Plantlets develop on base of each leaf blade. Variegated varieties are available.

Temperature: winter minimum 5°C (41°F). Avoid high winter temperature.
Humidity: mist occasionally.
Position: good light or semi-shade, not direct sun.
Watering and feeding: water freely from spring to autumn, sparingly in winter. Feed regularly in summer.
Care: if plant too large and stems congested, cut back in spring. Repot each spring.
Propagation: division; pot up plantlets.

TRADESCANTIA

Trailing foliage houseplants. Several variegated varieties with white or purple tinges.

Temperature: winter minimum 7°C (45°F).
Humidity: mist occasionally.
Position: good light, with some direct sun.
Watering and feeding: water freely from spring to autumn, sparingly in winter. Feed regularly from spring through to the autumn months.
Care: pinch out any unattractive shoots.
Propagation: cuttings.

TULIPA

Some tulips can
be forced for
winter colour.

Temperature: hardy.
Once in flower, the
cooler the room,
the longer the
flowers will last.
Humidity: unde-
manding.

Position: can be placed anywhere if
brought indoors just as flowers open.

Watering and feeding: water moderately
while in the home.

Care: in early or mid-autumn, plant bulbs
with necks just below soil. Place in
sheltered place outdoors and cover with
fine gravel or other suitable mulch at least
5 cm (2 in) deep. Keep soil in pots moist
but not overwatered. When shoots are 4–5
cm (1½–2 in) tall, place in light at about
15°C (59°F) until buds show colour. Bring
into the home. Discard or plant in garden
after flowering.

Propagation: buy fresh bulbs each year.

VRIESEA SPLENDENS

Bromeliad with
rosette of arch-
ing, strap-shaped,
banded leaves.
Bright red flower
bract in summer
and autumn.
Temperature:
winter minimum
15°C (59°F).

Humidity: mist leaves regularly.

Position: light shade or good light out of
direct sun.

Watering and feeding: water freely from
spring to autumn, sparingly in winter.
Keep "vase" of leaves topped up with
water from mid-spring to mid-autumn.
Soft water if possible. Feed a weak
fertilizer in summer.

Care: discard after flowering, or pot up
offsets in ericaceous soil.

Propagation: offsets.

YUCCA ELEPHANTIPES

Rosettes with
long pointed
leaves growing
from a trunk
section. Can
grow to ceiling.
Temperature:
winter minimum
7°C (45°F).
Humidity:
tolerates dry air.
Position: prefers
good light with
some sun but
avoid full sun.
Watering and

feeding: water freely from spring to
autumn, sparingly in winter.

Care: repot small plants as necessary, large
ones can remain in same container for
many years, but replace top 5 cm (2 in) of
potting soil.

Propagation: use sideshoots from the plant
as cuttings.

Displays & Groupings

YOU CAN CREATE A VARIETY OF DISPLAY EFFECTS BY CHOOSING PLANTS WITH DIFFERENT GROWTH HABITS AND SHAPES AND GROUPING THEM TOGETHER. EVEN THE PURCHASE OF A SINGLE PLANT CAN PROVIDE A WELCOME EVENT, ESPECIALLY WHEN IT BRIGHTENS UP THE DARKEST PART OF THE YEAR.

DISPLAYING PLANTS

Plants usually look better grouped together. Small plants can often be displayed more creatively arranged in planters or self-watering pots than in individual ones. You can even create miniature gardens.

Leaving larger plants in their individual pots, however, allows you to create different effects. You can also alter displays to suit changing seasons, or to accommodate seasonal highs and lows of some plants and to incorporate those in flower.

Above: Give a group of pots a sense of height by raising one at the back.

Sometimes a large plant is best viewed in isolation, so that its very size and importance will be emphasized. For instance, a 1.8 m (6 ft) tall yucca or a variegated *Ficus benjamina* that almost reaches the ceiling really need to be shown off without any competition from plants nearby.

When displaying plants in individual pots, the relationship of size and proportion between plant and pot can be a crucial factor. A mixture of mound-forming or trailing plants with upright ones tends to give equal prominence to plants and pots.

Plants with a cascading habit create a totally different effect, with containers

Above: A large plant is best viewed in isolation to be fully appreciated.

54

receding in importance. To make sure that the group doesn't lack a sense of height, you can raise one of the pots at the back.

Houseplants tend to grow slowly and are cultivated in a range of sizes. If a room requires a large plant, select one at the right height. Otherwise you could wait a long time for a 90 cm (3 ft) specimen to reach the necessary size.

Above: The formal symmetry of these two ivies creates a charming foreground to the garden beyond.

DISPLAY

Try to avoid placing all your plants at the same height – on tables and windowsills – as this will look predictable. Stand large specimens on the floor, or hang containers in light corners. Use trailing plants on the mantelpiece or from high shelving to show them at their best.

Containers should never dominate, but they can improve plants and many are ornaments in their own right. Choose them to complement the style of the room as well as the plant.

BACKGROUNDS

Plants are usually best viewed against a plain background. If you have a patterned wall-covering, the plants need to have big leaves, and plain green would be a definite advantage over those with variegated or coloured foliage.

Consider, too, how plants can look at night, for they can be attractively lit. Spotlights or uplighters will highlight plants and can be used to create interesting shadows on wall and ceilings.

GROUPS OR SINGLE SPECIMENS

Most plants prefer to grow in groups as they benefit from the microclimate produced, and three or four plants in a large container will make a greater impact than they would if dotted around the room.

Even using a single large container will add to a room's overall design. Large plants can generally be used in isolation, and many of the tall growers have enough presence to stand alone as a focal point.

Above: The compact rounded growth of Soleirolia soleirolii *is perfectly contained in a narrow wicker basket.*

The Right Plant for the Right Place

THE DIFFERENT ROOMS IN YOUR HOME PROVIDE A WHOLE RANGE OF
ENVIRONMENTS AND DÉCORS. CHOOSE PLANTS THAT WILL ENHANCE
THE STYLE AND MOOD OF A ROOM AND WILL THRIVE THERE.

THE LIVING ROOM

The living room is probably the best room in the home for growing houseplants. There are usually large windows and lots of standing places such as windowsills, tables, ledges and shelves.

Here, the colours and textures of plants play important roles, especially the way in which they blend or contrast with the background. Try to juxtapose contrasting forms, shapes and colours to emphasize the visual impact of the plants.

Plant Choices

Plants that like bright light, but not direct sunlight, such as aglaenemas, often do well by a window with net curtains. White net curtains make a good backdrop for many plants. Large specimen plants are excellent for living rooms because they provide strong focal points in any type of interior.

Colour Highlights

Seasonal flowers, such as spring bulbs, primulas and any of the flowering pot plants, can be used to create a focal point or draw attention to a particular object.

Exotic flowers always add sophistication and look good on coffee tables, shelves and mantelpieces. Larger flowering specimens can be displayed on a pedestal or plant stand to show them off to the full.

You might want to use an especially beautiful container as a cache-pot for an appropriately impressive plant like an azalea in full flower. As the blooms on one flowering plant die, replace it with another, so that your special corner of the room always looks fresh and colourful.

Left: A large, bright plant such as this Strelitzia reginae *makes a dramatic display in a neutral-coloured living room.*

Variegated plants, such as *Coleus blumei* hybrids, look good grouped together. Their distinctive patterns in warm pinks and reds are all good living room colours. Match the container with the plants.

Humidity

A major problem in living rooms is the effect of central heating, as many tropical houseplants dislike dry heat. Place vulnerable pots on a layer of wet pebbles in a tray. You can also hang small, relatively inexpensive humidifiers on radiators, with a shelf on top for plants.

THE KITCHEN

Modern kitchens are usually light and bright and relatively spacious. Plants should thrive here, and there should be plenty of opportunities for siting them. Your choice of plants, however, will be governed by the ambient temperature of the kitchen.

The windowsill is the first place to fill. Here you can grow those that need good light, but if it receives hot sun, you will be restricted to those that can cope, such as cacti, succulents, pelargoniums (geraniums) and tradescantias. Spring bulbs are also good here.

Open shelving near a window can be used for trailing plants, although watering can be a problem. Check on how much sun they can take. Avoid trailing plants near work surfaces or eating areas. Upright plants will be a better choice.

Right: The kitchen is an ideal place for a small container filled with culinary herbs.

For open shelves, or a unit dividing the dining area from the kitchen, compact, bushy plants are preferable to trailing ones. Good hanging plants include ferns and vines.

Herbs

Many cooks like growing culinary herbs in the kitchen, but if you use them a lot, for example parsley, chives and mint, you will be better growing them elsewhere. Keep herbs in the kitchen that supply aroma, such as small pots of rosemary, sage and thyme, and create mood. Most herbs need good light, so the best place is near a bright window where they can also be easily watered.

Many supermarkets sell herbs in small pots, and this is a very easy way to buy basil, which has such a wonderful flavour when fresh.

BEDROOMS

Most bedrooms are kept cooler than living rooms, and this is an advantage for many plants. Winter-flowering plants in particular often last much longer in a cool atmosphere. With the wide range of short-term flowering plants available the year round, you can always find something that will complement your own particular style and colour scheme.

Bedrooms are also an excellent place for a collection of cacti and succulents, and for large, individual specimens of tolerant foliage plants, such as aspidistras, which are unlikely to become stressed if forgotten for a day or two.

If you can discipline yourself to water and mist them regularly, however, even delicate ferns will often do well in a bedroom because the air is usually more humid than in a hot living room. Remember, though, that they need to be placed in good indirect light in order to flourish.

Left: A large individual specimen, such as this Heliconia, makes a striking statement.

Light and Shade

A table near a window is the perfect position for plants. While bedside tables and dressing tables might look nice with a plant, these are usually placed where natural light levels are low. Be prepared to move long-term plants around, siting them for a week or two when they are at their prime, then swapping them with plants that have been in better light.

Fragrance

Plants with a fragrance, such as gardenias, jasmine or hyacinths can be especially pleasing in the bedroom. Be careful of placing too powerful a plant in a small room; too much scent can inhibit sleep.

Above: *Containers of hyacinths provide both scent and colour in the bedroom.*

BATHROOMS

The average bathroom experiences short periods of high temperature and high humidity and longer spells of cool conditions. In addition, they often have poor natural light. There may also be airborne chemicals from aerosols and sprays, and dust from talcum powder. However, many plants thrive in these conditions if their foliage is cleaned regularly.

Try to keep plants out of reach of splashes from the bath and washbasin. The back of the bath is not a good position, and light levels will be low. Make the most of the windowsill, for flowering plants like *cyclamen* and *exacum*. Where there are no free surfaces, fix wire or glass shelves to a wall that receives light.

Above: Ferns like warmth and humidity, and look pretty in front of a mirror.

Within the room use plants with tough foliage. Many tropical plants can thrive in bathroom conditions, and there are several that tolerate a low light level. Try *Aglaonema* and *Maranta leuconeura*. Delicate ferns will survive indirect light if they are given humidity and warmth. Frequent misting is essential and will help keep the fronds clear of powder and sprays. Avoid plants with hairy foliage.

Place aspidistras and asparagus in front of a mirror where they will receive reflected light. *Philodendron scandens* looks good hanging from a high shelf.

In a small bathroom with a skylight, try hanging containers with ivies, which will tolerate cooler conditions during winter. Good specimen plants for large bathrooms are *Cyperus*, which like a wet environment, *Fatsia japonica*, and the Swiss cheese plant (*Monstera deliciosa*).

Above: Put potted plants on the bathroom windowsill so they receive natural light.

Plants at Their Best

USE THIS LIST AS A QUICK REFERENCE GUIDE TO PLAN YOUR DISPLAYS OF HOUSEPLANTS FOR ALL-YEAR-ROUND INTEREST.

SPRING

PLANT	INTEREST
Anthurium scherzerianum (gl, ^)	flower, red
Begonia eliator hybrids (gl, ^)	flower, various colours
Billbergia nutans (gl, ^)	bract, pink
Browallia (gl, ^)	flower, purple, blue, white
Chrysanthemum (gl, ^)	flower, various colours
Clivia (gl, ^)	flower, orange, yellow
Columnea (gl, ^)	flower, red
Crocus (gl, ^)	flower, various colours
Fuchsia hybrids (gl, ^)	flower, various colours
Hibiscus (gl, ^)	flower, various colours
Hyacinthus (gl, ^)	flower, various colours
Hydrangea (gl, ^)	flower, various colours
Impatiens (gl, ^)	flower, various colours
Kalanchoe blossfeldania (gl, ^)	flower, various colours
Lilium (gl, ^)	flower, various colours
Narcissus hybrids (gl, ^)	flower, yellow, white
Primula obconica (gl, ^)	flower, various colours
Rhododendron x *obtusum* (gl, *)	flower, various colours
Rhododendron simsii (gl, *)	flower, various colours
Saintpaulia (gl, ^)	flower, various colours
Sparrmannia africana (gl, ^)	flower, white

Anthurium scherzerianum

Hyacinthus

SUMMER

PLANT	INTEREST
Achimenes hybrida (gl, ^)	flower, various colours
Aechmea fasciata (gl, ^)	flower/bract, blue to lilac/pinky
Begonia eliator hybrids (gl, ^)	flower, all colours
Browallia (gl, ^)	flower, purple, blue, white
Campanula isophylla (gl, ^)	flower, blue
Celosia cristata (gl, ^)	flower, red, yellow, orange, pink
Chrysanthemum (gl, ^)	flower, various colours
Eustoma grandiflorum (gl, ^)	flower, various colours
Fuchsia hybrids (gl, ^)	flower, various colours
Gardenia jasminoides (gl, ^)	flower, white, fragrant
Hibiscus (gl, ^)	flower, various colours
Hoya bella (gl, ^)	flower, white, fragrant
Impatiens (gl, ^)	flower, various colours
Jasminum officinale (gl, ^)	flower, white, fragrant
Kalanchoe blossfeldiana (gl, ^)	flower, various colours
Rosa chinensis minima (gl, ^)	flower, various colours
Saintpaulia (gl, ^)	flower, various colours
Sinningia speciosa (gl, ^)	flower, various colours
Stephanotis floribunda (gl, ^)	flower, white, fragrant
Streptocarpus hybrids (gl, ^)	flower, various colours
Vriesea splendens (ls, gl, ^)	bract, red

Browallia

Gardenia

AUTUMN

PLANT	INTEREST
Acalypha hispida (gl, ^)	flower, red
Aechmea fasciata (gl, ^)	flower/bract, blue to lilac/pink
Begonia eliator hybrids (gl, ^)	flower, all colours
Browallia (gl, ^)	flower, purple, blue, white
Chrysanthemum (u, ^)	flower, various colours
Colchicum autumnale (gl, ^)	flower, pink
Exacum affine (gl, ^)	flower, pale purple
Fuchsia hybrids (gl, ^)	flower, various colours
Hibiscus (gl, ^)	flower, various colours
Impatiens (gl, ^)	flower, various colours
Kalanchoe blossfeldania (gl, ^)	flower, various colours
Nertera granadensis (gl, ^)	berry, orange
Saintpaulia (gl, ^)	flower, various colours
Solanum capsicastrum (gl, ^)	berry, green
Vriesea splendens (ls, gl, ^)	bract, red

Acalypha hispida

WINTER

PLANT	INTEREST
Begonia eliator hybrids (gl, ^)	flower, all colours
Browallia (gl, ^)	flower, purple, blue, white
Chrysanthemum (u, ^)	flower, various colours
Columnea (gl, ^)	flower, red
Cyclamen (gl, ^)	flower, pastel colours
Erica gracilis (gl, ^)	flower, pink
Erica hyemalis (gl, ^)	flower, white, pink
Hyacinthus (gl, ^)	flower, various colours
Impatiens (gl, ^)	flower, various colours
Jasminum polyanthum (gl, ^)	flower, white
Kalanchoe blossfeldiana (gl, ^)	flower, various colours
Narcissus hybrids (gl, ^)	flower, yellow, white
Primula obconica (gl, ^)	flower, various colours
Rhododendron x obtusum (gl, *)	flower, various colours
Rhododendron simsii (gl,*)	flower, various colours
Saintpaulia (gl, ^)	flower, various colours
Solanum capsicastrum (bl, ^)	berry, red
Tulipa (a, ^)	flower, various colours

Cyclamen

Tulipa

SYMBOLS

gl = good light
bl = best light
ls = light shade
a = anywhere
u = undemanding

Plants marked with ^ prefer alkaline soil
Plants marked with * prefer acid soil

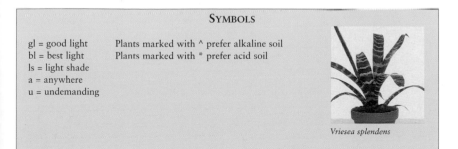

Vriesea splendens

Common Names of Plants

African violet *Saintpaulia*
Arabian violet *Exacum affine*
Azalea *Rhododendron simsii*
Asparagus fern *Asparagus densiflorus* 'Sprengeri'
Autumn crocus *Colchicum autumnale*
Barrel cactus *Echinocactus grusonii*
Bead plant *Nertera granadensis*
Bird's nest fern *Asplenium nidus*
Bush violet *Browallia speciosa*
Busy Lizzie *Impatiens*
Calamondin orange x *Citrofortunella microcarpa*
Canary date palm *Phoenix canariensis*
Cape heath *Erica gracilis*
Cape primrose *Streptocarpus hybrid*
Cast iron plant *Aspidistra elatior*
Chenille plant *Acalypha hispida*
Coconut palm *Cocos nucifera*
Croton *Codiaeum variegatum pictum*
Cupid's bower *Achimenes hybrida*
Devil's ivy *Epipremnum aureum*
Emerald fern *Asparagus densiflorus* 'Sprengeri'
English ivy *Hedera helix*
Gloxinia *Sinningia speciosa*
False aralia *Dizygotheca*
Flame nettle *Coleus blumei*
Flaming Katy *Kalanchoe blossfeldiana*
Flaming sword *Vriesea splendens*
Freckle face *Hypoestes*
Geranium *Pelargonium*
Grape ivy *Cissus rhombifolia*

Goldfish plant *Columnea*
Goosefoot plant *Syngonium podophyllum*
Hen-and-chicken fern *Asplenium bulbiferum*
House lime *Sparrmannia africana*
Hot water plant *Achimenes hybrida*
Japanese azalea *Rhododendron* x *obtusum*
Kaffir lily *Clivia miniata*
Pigtail plant *Anthurium scherzerianum*
Flamingo flower *Anthurium scherzerianum*
Living stones *Lithops*
Mind your own business *Soleirolia soleirolii*
Miniature wax plant *Hoya bella*
Mother fern *Asplenium bulbiferum*
Mother in law's tongue *Sansevieria trifasciata* 'Laurentii'
Pink jasmine *Jasminum polyanthum*
Poison primrose *Primula obconica*
Prairie gentian *Eustoma grandiflorum*
Queen's tears *Billbergia nutans*

Red-hot cat's tail *Acalypha hispida*
Red pineapple *Ananas bracteatus striatus*
Rosary vine *Ceropegia woodii*
Rose of china *Hibiscus sinensis*
Sentry palm *Howea belmoreana*
Spider plant *Chlorophytum comosum* 'Vittatum'
Spineless yucca *Yucca elephantipes*
Sweetheart plant *Philodendron scandens*
Swiss cheese plant *Monstera deliciosa*
Sword fern *Nephrolepis exaltata*
String of hearts *Ceropegia woodii*
Umbrella plant *Cyperus*
Urn plant *Aechmea fasciata*
Wax flower *Stephanotis floribunda*
Weeping fig *Ficus benjamina*
White jasmine *Jasminum officinale*
Winter cherry *Solanum capsicastrum*

Below: Hypoestes Phyllostachya

62

Index

Index